♀ Emma Watson

Women's Rights Activist

by Kate Moening

BLASTOFF! READERS
2

BELLWETHER MEDIA • MINNEAPOLIS, MN

Note to Librarians, Teachers, and Parents:

Blastoff! Readers are carefully developed by literacy experts and combine standards-based content with developmentally appropriate text.

Level 1 provides the most support through repetition of high-frequency words, light text, predictable sentence patterns, and strong visual support.

Level 2 offers early readers a bit more challenge through varied simple sentences, increased text load, and less repetition of high-frequency words.

Level 3 advances early-fluent readers toward fluency through increased text and concept load, less reliance on visuals, longer sentences, and more literary language.

Level 4 builds reading stamina by providing more text per page, increased use of punctuation, greater variation in sentence patterns, and increasingly challenging vocabulary.

Level 5 encourages children to move from "learning to read" to "reading to learn" by providing even more text, varied writing styles, and less familiar topics.

Whichever book is right for your reader, Blastoff! Readers are the perfect books to build confidence and encourage a love of reading that will last a lifetime!

This edition first published in 2020 by Bellwether Media, Inc.

No part of this publication may be reproduced in whole or in part without written permission of the publisher. For information regarding permission, write to Bellwether Media, Inc., Attention: Permissions Department, 6012 Blue Circle Drive, Minnetonka, MN 55343.

Library of Congress Cataloging-in-Publication Data

Names: Moening, Kate, author.
Title: Emma Watson : Women's Rights Activist / by Kate Moening
Description: Minneapolis, MN : Bellwether Media, Inc., 2020. | Series: Blastoff! Readers : women leading the way | Includes bibliographical references and index. | Audience: Ages: 5-8. | Audience: Grades: K-3. | Summary: Relevant images match informative text in this introduction to Emma Watson. Intended for students in kindergarten through third grade"– Provided by publisher.
Identifiers: LCCN 2019024659 (print) | LCCN 2019024660 (ebook) | ISBN 9781644871201 (library binding) | ISBN 9781618917966 (paperback) | ISBN 9781618917768 (ebook)
Subjects: LCSH: Watson, Emma, 1990–Juvenile literature. | Actresses–Great Britain–Biography–Juvenile literature. | Feminists–Great Britain–Biography–Juvenile literature.
Classification: LCC PN2598.W25 M64 2020 (print) | LCC PN2598.W25 (ebook) | DDC 791.4302/8092 [B]–dc23
LC record available at https://lccn.loc.gov/2019024659
LC ebook record available at https://lccn.loc.gov/2019024660

Text copyright © 2020 by Bellwether Media, Inc. BLASTOFF! READERS and associated logos are trademarks and/or registered trademarks of Bellwether Media, Inc.

Editor: Al Albertson   Designer: Andrea Schneider

Printed in the United States of America, North Mankato, MN.

Table of Contents

Who Is Emma Watson?

Emma Watson is an actor and **activist**. She is most famous for playing Hermione in the Harry Potter movies.

Emma also fights for women's rights. She believes **feminism** is important!

Emma in *Harry Potter and the Prisoner of Azkaban*

"DON'T LET ANYONE TELL YOU WHAT YOU CAN AND CAN'T DO." (2015)

Emma was born in France.
Her parents **divorced** when
she was young.

Oxfordshire, England
Emma's hometown

Emma moved to England
with her mom and brother.

Getting Her Start

Young Emma loved to learn.
She also acted in school plays.

When Emma was 9,
she **auditioned** to play
Hermione. She won the part!

Emma Watson Profile

Birthday: April 15, 1990

Hometown:
Oxfordshire, England

Field: film, activism

Schooling:
- **studied English**
  literature

Influences:
- **Jacqueline Luesby**
  (mother)
- **Gloria Steinem**
  (women's rights activist)

Fans loved Emma. But it was hard to grow up famous.

Emma wanted to be out of the spotlight. She moved to the United States for college.

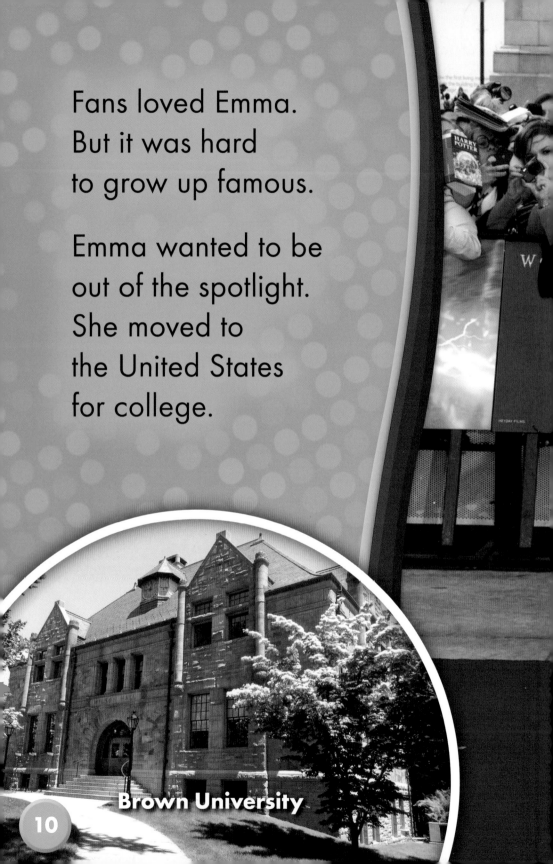

Brown University

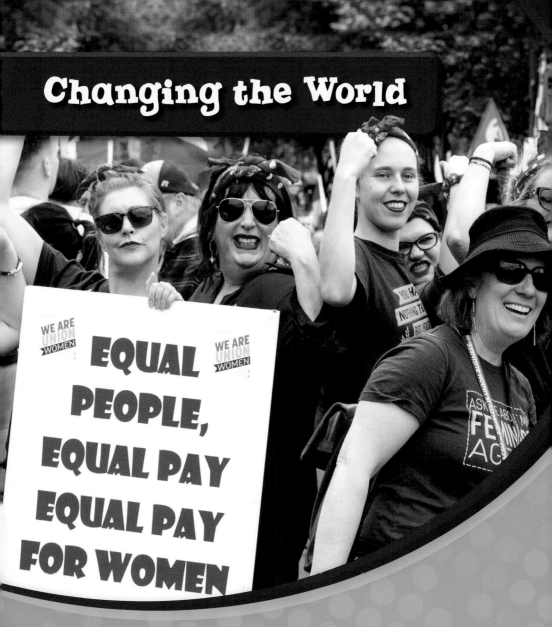

Emma saw **inequality** in the world. Women are often paid less than men.

Girls in many countries
cannot go to school.
Emma had to speak out!

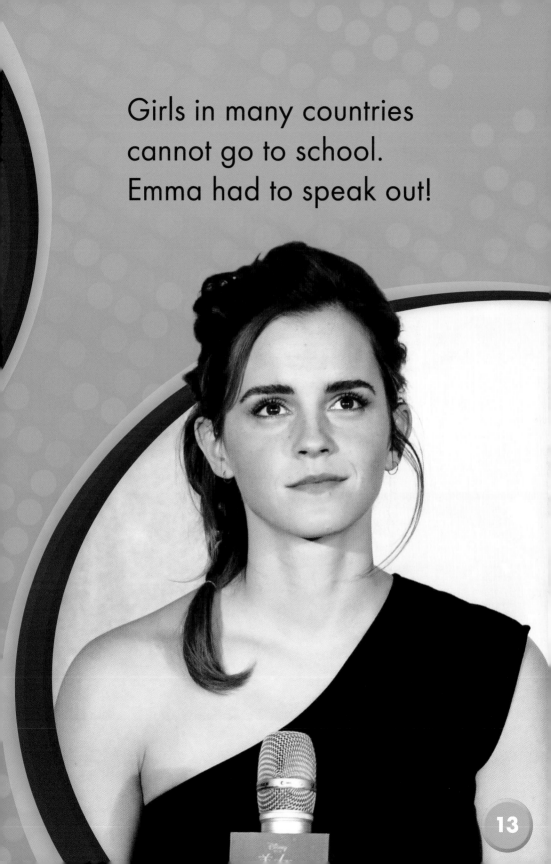

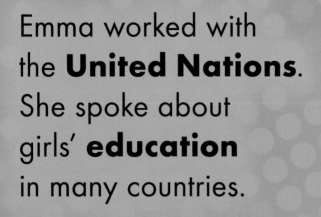

Emma worked with
the **United Nations**.
She spoke about
girls' **education**
in many countries.

She started a **campaign**.
She wanted both men
and women to fight
for women's rights!

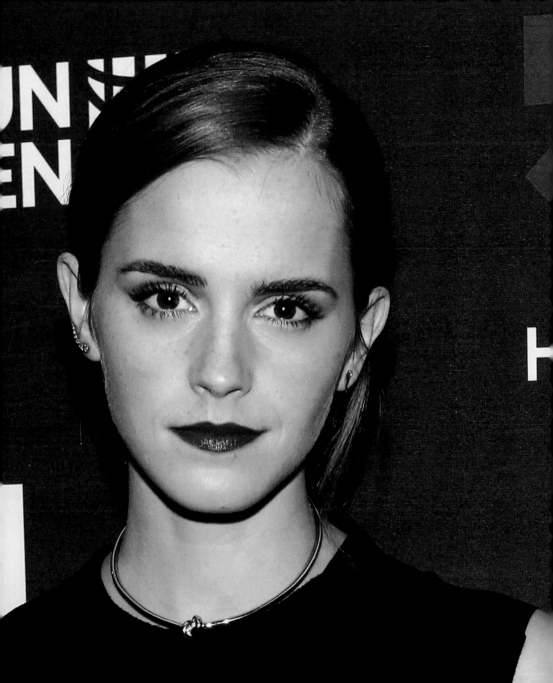

Emma working on her HeForShe campaign

Many people did not want Emma to speak up. Sometimes she got **threats**.

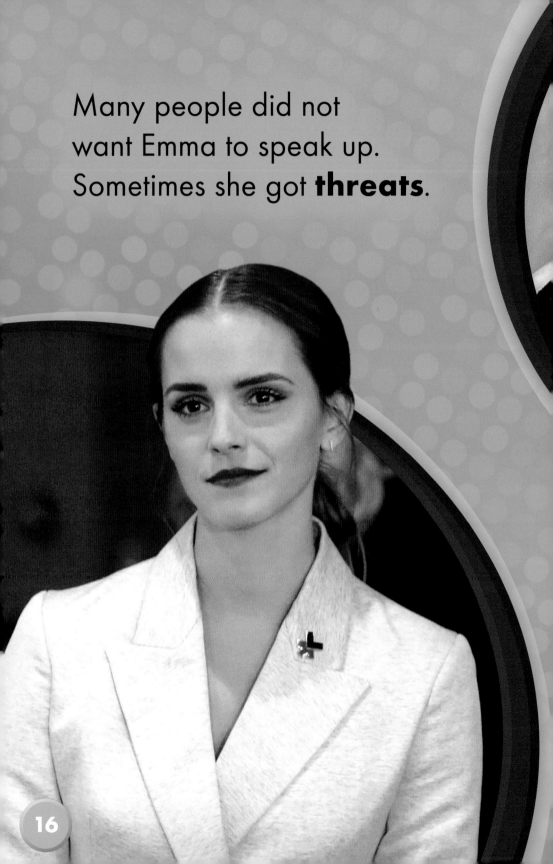

But Emma was brave!
Other activists helped her
stay strong.

Emma's Future

Today, Emma continues to act!
She is still an activist, too.

Emma Watson Timeline

1999	Emma is cast as Hermione in *Harry Potter and the Sorcerer's Stone*
2014	Emma begins work with the United Nations
2014	Emma starts the HeForShe campaign for gender equality
2015	Emma is named one of *Time* magazine's "100 Most Influential People"

Emma knows there is always more to learn.

Emma plans to keep teaching people about feminism.

She wants everyone to be free to use their voice!

Emma attending the 2017 Women's March

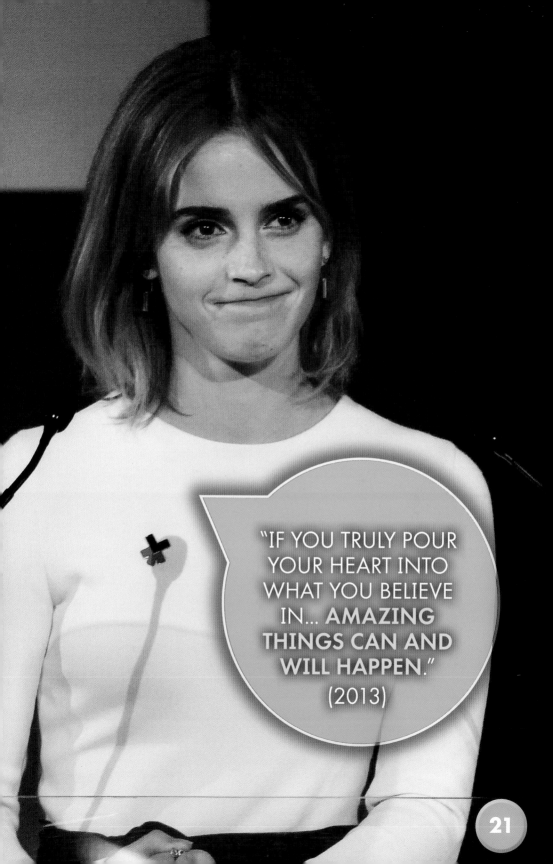

Glossary

activist—a person who believes in taking action to make changes in laws or society

auditioned—tried out for a role

campaign—a connected series of activities that work to bring about a particular event

divorced—separated and stopped being married

education—the knowledge, skill, and understanding that a person gets from going to school

feminism—the belief that people of all genders should have equal rights and opportunities

inequality—the lack of just or fair treatment for all groups

threats—statements saying a person will be harmed if they do not do what someone wants them to do

United Nations—a world organization that works toward peace between countries

To Learn More

AT THE LIBRARY

Halligan, Katherine. *HerStory: 50 Women and Girls Who Shook Up the World*. New York, N.Y.: Simon & Schuster Books for Young Readers, 2018.

Lajiness, Katie. *Emma Watson: Talented Actress*. Minneapolis, Minn.: Abdo Publishing, 2018.

Moening, Kate. *Malala Yousafzai: Education Activist*. Minneapolis, Minn.: Bellwether Media, 2019.

ON THE WEB

FACTSURFER

Factsurfer.com gives you a safe, fun way to find more information.

1. Go to www.factsurfer.com.

2. Enter "Emma Watson" into the search box and click 🔍.

3. Select your book cover to see a list of related web sites.

Index